AN INTRODUCTION TO
RENEWABLE ENERGY SOURCES

ENVIRONMENT BOOKS FOR KIDS
Children's Environment Books

BABY PROFESSOR
EDUCATION KIDS

Speedy Publishing LLC
40 E. Main St. #1156
Newark, DE 19711
www.speedypublishing.com

In this book, we're going to talk about renewable energy sources. So, let's get right to it!

Power generating factories in the mountains.

WHAT IS NON-RENEWABLE ENERGY?

In order to power our cars, homes, and factories, we need sources of energy. Some of these sources of energy will run out if we overuse them. For example, coal is a type of fuel called a fossil fuel. It takes millions of years for coal to form in the Earth. The coal that is being used today was created from plants that died millions of years ago. Once coal is mined from the Earth, then it can't be replaced so it's a non-renewable form of energy.

Petroleum that is used to create gasoline for powering cars and natural gas that is used for heating are also fossil fuels and are non-renewable forms of energy as well.

Oil pipeline in industrial district with factories at dusk.

All of these fuels were created by a similar process. Many millions of years ago, the Earth was covered with very dense, swamp-like forests and large seas that were quite shallow. Plants on land, as well as algae and plankton in water, thrived in these wet environments. When they died, the stored energy from their chlorophyll was buried in the mud.

They were crushed under layers of rocks and sediment under very great amounts of pressure and heat. Eventually, after millions of years, they turned into large underground reservoirs of fossil fuels.

Because the process of creating non-renewable sources of energy takes millions upon millions of years, if we use up and deplete these resources on Earth, they will not exist anymore.

Oil pump.

Fossil fuels are fairly inexpensive to obtain from the ground through mining and they can be shipped where they are needed. This is why they were used for so long and other alternative energy sources weren't sought. For centuries, no one thought too much about what would happen if all these fuels were used up, because they thought the Earth was so large that they wouldn't run out.

Oil Refinery.

Things changed when it was discovered that the burning of these fuels was causing a lot of pollution. When they are burned, they create carbon dioxide as a by-product. When too much CO_2 is released into the air, it causes something called the *"Greenhouse Effect."* If you've ever been inside a greenhouse, you would know that it's quite hot. When too much CO_2 is released, it heats up the Earth's atmosphere causing dangerous global warming.

Smokestacks with pollution.

If this warming continues or gets worse, most scientists believe that the consequences will be disastrous. These consequences could include a huge change in Earth's climate and a significant rise in the sea levels as the Earth warms and ice melts. It will also cause very extreme weather events, such as devastating hurricanes, tornadoes, and massive floods. Ocean waters will become more acidic, which will have a large impact on animal and plant life.

Polar bear on ice close to golden glittering water.

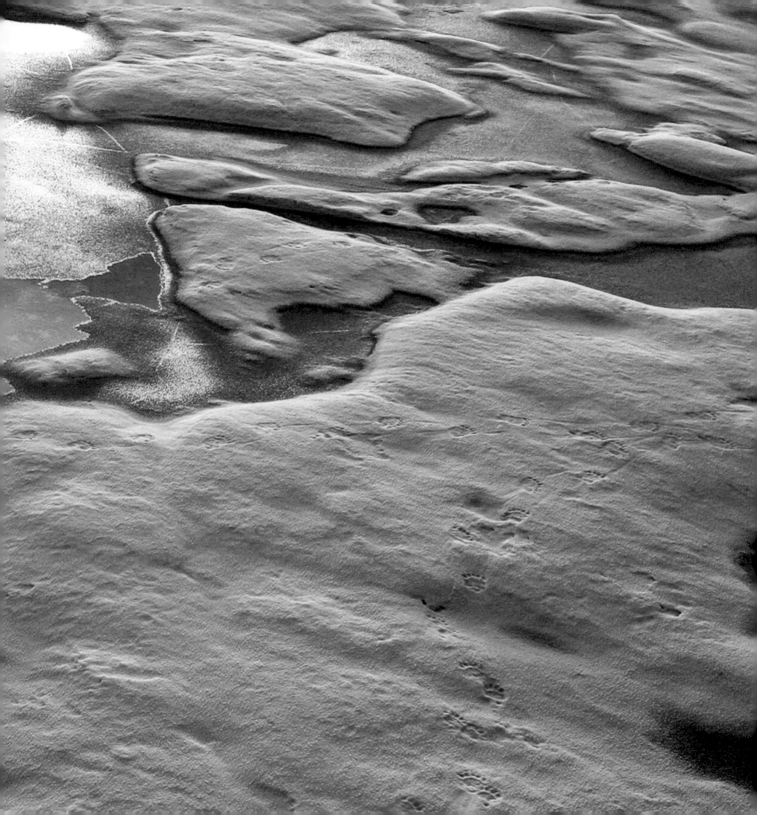

CAN THE GREENHOUSE EFFECT STILL BE REVERSED?

Many scientists believe that it's too late to stop global warming from happening. If that's the case, there are only a few options.

- Don't change and just live with the consequences. Continue to use non-renewable sources of energy.

- Get used to the altered climate, which will more than likely be very extreme in many cases.

- Start limiting the use of fossil fuels so that the CO_2 in the atmosphere will begin to get back into a normal balance.

If we choose to take a more active approach, then we will need different sources of energy so that we're not burning fossil fuels anymore.

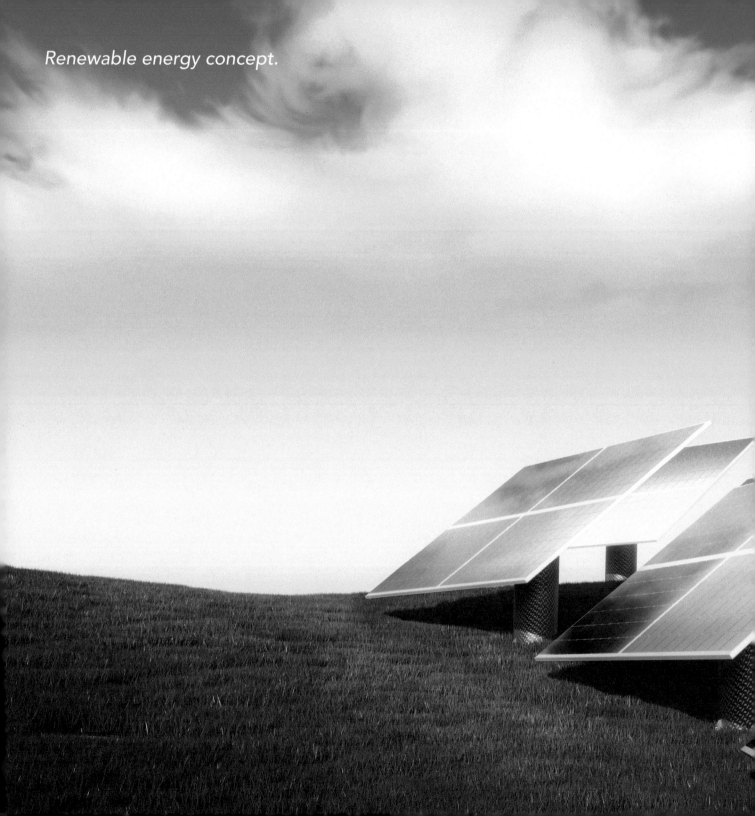
Renewable energy concept.

WHAT IS RENEWABLE ENERGY?

There are many different types of renewable energy and scientists are still inventing ways to make the best use of them. Renewable energy is the exact opposite of non-renewable energy. These types of energy sources depend on sources that will always be with us.

For example, there will always be wind on Earth. If we use wind to generate electricity, it won't be used up at any point. If an energy source can't be permanently *"used up,"* then it is a renewable source. Most renewable energy sources don't emit harmful polluting chemicals into the air or water, so they are also called *"Green Energy."*

Solar panels with wind turbines.

Wind Turbines.

THE MAJOR TYPES OF RENEWABLE ENERGY SOURCES

Nature has immense power and there are many ways to tap into energy that doesn't require the emission of dangerous CO2.

WIND-POWERED ENERGY

Windmills and other types of wind turbines have been constructed for more than 1,000 years. However, they were never used in vast numbers to generate power. They were generally used for pumping water or as a means to grind grain. Today, modern wind-powered turbines take the kinetic energy from the fast-moving wind and transform it into electricity.

Of course, wind turbines can't work well unless the conditions are just right for them to generate electricity. They have to have wind that is moving at a speed of about 14 miles per hour to work well and if the wind is too powerful they can be damaged.

Solar energy panels with wind turbines.

SOLAR ENERGY

There are different ways that energy from the Sun can be harnessed. You may have seen solar panels on the top of a house or have some on your own house. The reason these panels are on rooftops is because this is where they will receive the most sunlight. Solar panels allow the photons in light to interact with a *"Silicon Sandwich"* inside each solar cell of the panel. Within the solar cell, there are two layers of silicon crystals that have been treated to react in different ways.

Solar panel installation.

As sunlight hits the top layer of the crystals of silicon, it gets the electrons in the atoms moving. The top layer wants to get rid of those electrons to become stable again. The bottom layer of silicon is treated so it wants those electrons to come to it, so it can become stable. The electrons begin moving from the top layer to the bottom layer, and electricity is created by this movement.

Traditional american home with modern solar panels on roof.

HYDROPOWER

Creating energy through the use of water is currently the most used of the renewable forms of energy. The energy of moving water is very powerful. The water in natural falls or manmade dams can be harnessed so that its kinetic energy is converted to electrical energy. For example, a large manmade dam holds water.

Hydroelectric Power Station Turbines, Hoover Dam Fuel and Power Generation.

Gates control how much water is let out into pipes. The water has potential energy that becomes kinetic energy as it speeds through the pipes. The high speed of the water turns generator shafts to create electrical power.

Water rushing out of hydro dam.

GEOTHERMAL POWER

Under the surface of the Earth there is a lot of heat. Scientists don't yet have a way to harness the heat from the molten rock called magma, which is under the Earth's surface. However, there are places where the layers of rock are pretty hot close to the Earth's surface. Wells are dug down where there are reservoirs of hot water.

Geothermal Power Station.

The water is pumped up under a high amount of pressure. Then, the pressure is dropped when the water gets closer to the surface. This causes the water to produce hot steam. The power from the steam turns a turbine. Motion from the spinning turbine transforms the kinetic energy into electrical energy.

Geothermal Power Station, Turkey.

BIOMASS ENERGY

This type of energy comes from animals and plants that were once alive. Dead vegetation, dead wood and wood products, leftovers from crops, some types of garbage, and aquatic plants that are processed from the ocean are all potential items that can be converted to biomass energy. These items have energy trapped inside them and if they are burned it can be converted to usable energy.

Bio power plant with storage of wooden fuel.

For example, wood is useful as a biomass fuel. If we replace trees that are cut down with new ones quickly enough, then wood is a renewable resource. As was true for fossil fuels, if the material is plant-based then its original energy came from the sun. When these items are burned, they create steam and the steam drives turbines to produce electricity.

Pellets-Biomas.

Another type of biomass energy is ethanol fuel. It's created from crops that contain a lot of sugar such as corn. Ethanol can be used in place of gasoline.

Biomass power plant.

Wind Power in the sea of clouds, Guilin, China.

FASCINATING FACTS ABOUT RENEWABLE ENERGY

- Wind-powered energy is becoming a very fast-growing type of energy source.

- The largest wind turbine in the world is located in Maade, Denmark. It has propellers that are 263 feet long. In just one day of operation it can produce a month's worth of power for hundreds of average-sized homes.

- If harnessed, the sunlight that hits the Earth for just one hour would be enough to meet the world's total energy demands for one solid year.

- By 2050, scientists predict that solar power will be the world's most important source of renewable energy.

Electric power generation.

- Even though magma can't be used directly yet, most geothermal plants are located near the *"Ring of Fire,"* which is where most of the volcanoes and earthquakes on Earth occur. This is because the water underground is naturally hotter in those areas.

Awesome! Now you know more about the different types of renewable energy sources. You can find more Environment books from Baby Professor by searching the website of your favorite book retailer.

Made in the USA
Columbia, SC
03 August 2024

39937459R00038